¿Cuánto es un par?
How Many Is A Pair?

Ted R. Schaefer
traducido por Héctor Viana

Rourke
Publishing LLC
Vero Beach, Florida 32964

www.rourkepublishing.com

PHOTO CREDITS: © Armentrout: pages 4, 5, 7, 9, 11, 12, 20, 21; © Bradley Mason: page 6; © Rob Friedman: page 10; © Corel: page 13; © Franky DeMeyer: page 14; © Kenn Kiser: page 19

Editor: Robert Stengard-Olliges

Cover design by Nicola Stratford.

Library of Congress Cataloging-in-Publication Data

Schaefer, Ted, 1948-
  Cuanto es un Par (How many is a pair?) / Ted Schaefer.
      p. cm. -- (My first math 500 Includes index.)
    ISBN 1-60044-284-6
  1. Binary system (Mathematics)--Juvenile literature. 2.
Counting--Juvenile literature. I. Title.

Printed in the USA

CG/CG

Rourke Publishing

www.rourkepublishing.com – sales@rourkepublishing.com
Post Office Box 3328, Vero Beach, FL 32964

11 08

Contenido
Table of Contents

Tenis
Running Shoes

Llevo puesto mi **par** de tenis favorito.

I am wearing my favorite **pair** of running shoes.

¿Cuántos hay en un *par*? Cuenta los tenis.

How many is a *pair*? Count the shoes.

Un par son dos. / A pair is two.

Hoy corro con las gemelas.

Today, I race with the twins.

¿Cuántas gemelas hay? Cuenta las chicas.

How many people make twins? Count the girls.

Gemelas son dos personas. / Twins are two people.

Triciclos
Tricycles

Montamos en triciclo.

We race our tricycle.

Tri significa tres. / Tri means three.

How many does **tri** mean? Count the wheels?

¿Qué número significa **tri**? Cuenta las ruedas.

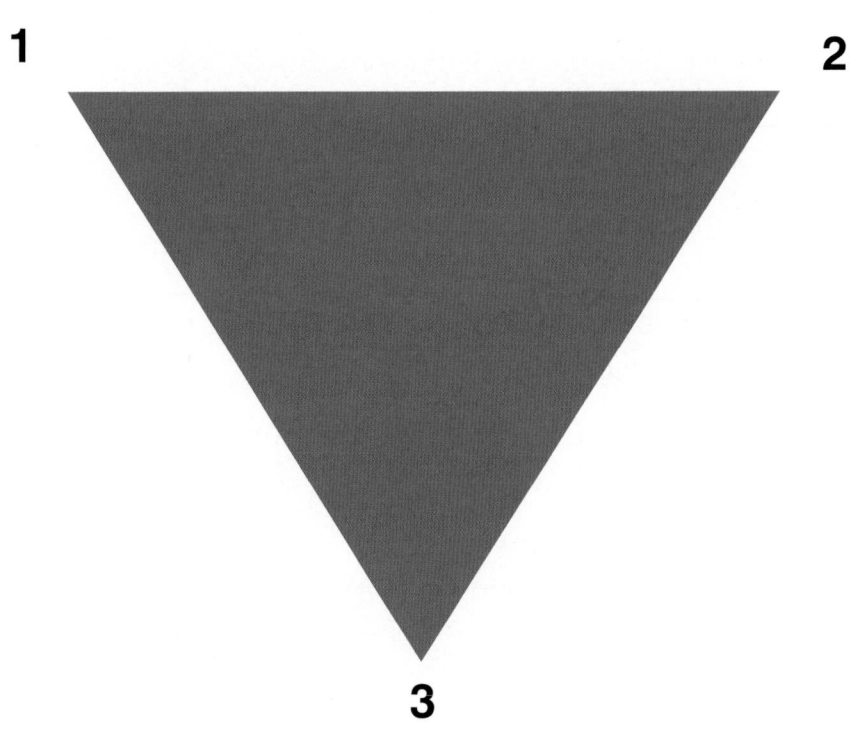

1   **2**

3

Cuenta y verás. Si *tri* significa tres…
entonces un triángulo tiene tres lados

Count and see. If *tri* means three...
then a triangle has three sides

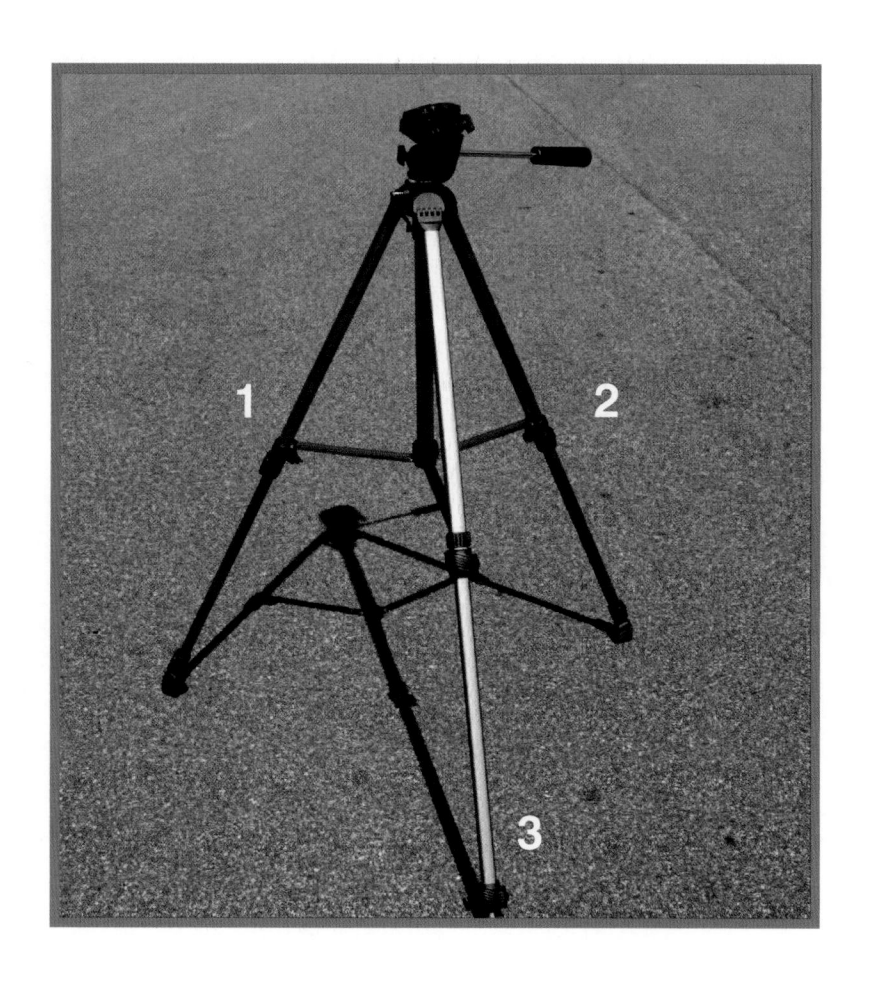

y un trípode tiene tres patas.

and a tripod has three legs.

Montamos en bicicleta.

We race bicycles.

Bi significa dos. / Bi means two.

How many does **bi** mean? Count the wheels.

¿Qué número significa **bi**? Cuenta las ruedas.

Cuenta y verás. Si *bi* significa dos…
entonces los binoculares tienen dos tubos

Count and see. If *bi* means two…
then binoculars have two tubes

y un biplano tiene dos juegos de alas.

and a biplane has two sets of wings.

Un par de bancos
A Pair Of Benches

Nos sentamos y descansamos en un **par** de bancos. ¿Qué número significa "un par"? Cuenta los bancos.

We sit and rest on a **pair** of benches. How many does a "pair" mean? Count the benches.

Un par son dos. / A pair is two.

Un hombre monta en monociclo. ¿Qué número significa **mono**? Cuenta las ruedas.

A man rides past us on a unicycle. How many does **uni** mean? Count the wheel.

Mono significa uno. / Uni means one.

Uni también significa uno.
Cuenta y verás. Si *uni* significa uno…
entonces la música al unísono tiene un solo sonido.

Count and see. If *uni* means one...
then music in unison has one sound.

Un uniforme es una ropa igual para todos.

A uniform is one set of clothes for everyone to wear.

Me siento para descansar mi par de pies cansados. Aaaaaaah.

I sit and rest my pair of tired feet. Aaaaaaah.

Glosario / Glossary

bi — dos
bi (BYE) — two

par — dos cosas
pair (PAIR) — two of something

tri — tres
tri (TRY) — three

mono/uni — uno
uni (u NEE) — one

Índice

Index

Lecturas adicionales / Further Reading

Ball, Johnny. *Go Figure!* DK, 2005.
Glicksman, Caroline. *Eric the Math Bear.* Random House, 2003.
Pistoia, Sara. *Counting.* Child's World, 2003.

Sitios web para visitar / Websites To Visit

pbskids.org/cyberchase/parentsteachers/index.html
www.coolmath-games.com/numbermonster/index.html
www.coolmath4kids.com/coloringbook.html

Sobre el autor / About The Author

Ted Schaefer es autor y carpintero. Cuando no investiga para escribir sus libros informativos para niños, construye muebles en su taller.

Ted Schaefer is both a writer and a woodworker. When he isn't researching and writing informational books for children, he is building furniture in his shop.